The ... ue
Histo... ory

Mary R. Anderson

INFOA

Arrival of Slavs in Moravia and Bohemia

5th - 6th century

German tribes were forced out and thence arose the first empire - Sámo's Empire

ISBN 80-7240-032-0

The Stones of Prague

History, Pattern and Memory

Mary R. Anderson

Illustrations
Zdeněk Netopil

Prague
and Berkeley
1998

INFOA

***Mary R. Anderson, Ph.D.**, Professor of History at Holy Names College, Oakland, California, earned her doctorate from the University of California at Berkeley with a specialization in 19th and 20th century European Intellectual History. Dr. Anderson has participated in scholarly conferences and seminars throughout the United States, and in Russia, Denmark and the Czech Republic. She has lived in both Paris and London. Her work has earned numerous grants and awards, including three grants from the National Endowment for the Humanities and a biographical sketch in THE WORLD WHO'S WHO OF WOMEN. Her love of Prague inspired this journey into its history.*

The Stones of Prague
History, Pattern and Memory

Mary R. Anderson

As I found myself writing "a good likeness" across a lithograph of Prague, I realized that the city had become for me a person. If Paris is a beautiful woman always on display, Prague is the dowager empress always present - "always here and always now." [1]

The empress began life in the fourth century B.C. in Celtic tribes known as the Bois in Bohemia and the Cotins in Moravia.[2] But it was centuries before her streets

[1] *Attributed to Juliana of Norwich (1343-1416? 1419?). According to Jim Conlon, Director of the Sophia Institute at Holy Names College in Oakland, California, on 13 May 1373 Juliana was 30 and one-half years old. Dr. Conlon establishes her death as between 1416 and 1419.*

[2] *Jaroslav Krejčíř and Stanislav Soják, CZECH HISTORY (Prague, 1996), 5.*

began to speak in a language the historian could understand. This book has four interrelated purposes: 1) to examine in a highly condensed version some of the highlights of Czech history which has remained a relatively obscure field for Western historians until recently; 2) to see in the historical problem of periodization the additional insights and interplay between events which can be found; 3) to discern historical patterns in Czech history, most of which are still with us at the end of the twentieth century; and 4) to listen poetically and critically to the language of the stones of Prague, with the knowledge that even today cobblestone is not an easy language to read.

The stones spoke first in the language of music in words accented deliberately to nuance the rise and fall, the pauses and emphases in human conversation.[3] Perhaps this nuancing is an inherent function of language itself, but for the dowager empress city (a portrait which can only emerge as we proceed), the beautifully nuanced Czech language left one of the world's greatest musical

[3] *Conversations with Czech scholar and professional musician Laurence S. Oppenheim, September 1996.*

treasure troves. In these early centuries after the fall of the Roman Empire in the West, Prague's stones recorded Charlemagne's expedition to Bohemia in 805 resulting in the Christianization of the entire Central European area. Even then, presaging divisive issues centuries in advance, a struggle emerged between those who adhered to a Latin liturgy and those who favored a Slavic liturgy which Prague's people could understand. In 973 the Prague Diocese was founded as part of the Roman Catholic Church. With official Church recognition, the Bohemian state entered the realm of "Christendom" always more an ideal than a reality.

More to the point politically, the first decades of the eleventh century saw the rise of a Polish-Czech realm in a world of Realpolitik. By the thirteenth century, the Czech king was one of the seven electors of the Holy Roman Empire, founded by the Germanic kings from the remains of Charlemagne's empire. Centuries later, Voltaire would characterize this political anomoly as neither Holy nor Roman nor Empire. The political machinations of these centuries included Papal pretensions to rule over a geographical "Christendom" embracing all of Europe. Indeed vestiges of these aims remained for centuries as the Papal States in the Italian peninsula endured until the unification of Italy in 1870. In this earlier age Pope Celestine III (1191-1198), acting like any other feudal lord, gave both Bohemia and Moravia as a fief to the Bishop of Prague in 1192. The feudal centuries in the Czech lands were typical of European feudalism in general, with the pageantry of erecting castles, fortifying emerging towns and colonizing boundary forests, including the usual result of blood-letting covered by a chivalric cloak and the equally usual confusion between church and state. Dynasties were often built on flimsy, ever-shifting political grounds. The one constant remained Hapsburg attempts to gain the Bohemian crown. Following the slaying of the last Bohemian ruler of the House of Přemyslid after a 400-year reign and a fresh incursion into Poland in 1306, Albrecht I, King of Rome, proclaimed the dynasty's death and reserved the crown of Bohemia for his son, Rudolf of Hapsburg.

But with Rudolph's early death in battle, contending nobles again sought the crown until Karel IV (1326-

1378), son of Jan Lucemburský who ruled both as King of Bohemia and Emperor of Rome, ascended the throne initiating a Golden Age of art, literature and architecture. In spite of the Black Death of 1348 which carried off at least 30% of the population of Europe, Karel IV's reign saw the foundation of the New City of Prague, the beginning of construction of St. Vitus Cathedral (still one of the jewels of European culture) and the foundation of Prague University, oddly enough in the great plague year itself. Construction of a new stone bridge over the Vltava River begun in 1357 witnesses today to the Czech sense of history with the western tower of the original bridge preserved as part of the new structure.[4] Flood

[4] *The historical framework throughout this paper has been adapted from Krejčíř and Soják, op. cit.; Bohumír Mráz, PRAGUE: THE HEART OF EUROPE (Prague, 1992); Tim Porter, PRAGUE: ART AND HISTORY (Prague, 1995); Hana Bílková and Jiří Šourek, PRAGUE: A PHOTOGRAPHIC GUIDE (Prague, 1995) and lectures by Dr. Peter Griffin of Oxford University (London: University Vacations, 1996. "700. Prague: The Jewel of Bohemia," 1-7 September 1996). Personal observations draw on extended visits to Prague in 1995 and 1996.*

waters of the Vltava had necessitated a higher structure, and this new bridge of the fourteenth century, with its famous statuary dating from the eighteenth century, is today one of Europe's grandest sights. Likewise attesting to the Czech sense of history in this dowager empress city is Karel's tomb in St. Vitus Cathedral which, in contrast to the Hapsburg tombs' long lists of accomplishments, bears the simple name "Karel." In 1356 the Golden Charter of Karel IV provided for election of the Holy Roman Emperor by majority of the Germanic kings with the prime place reserved for the King of Bohemia. Unfortunately, fratricidal wars followed Karel IV's death in 1378, destroying Czech hegemony in Central Europe.

Meanwhile, the Bohemian reformer Jan Hus had begun to question the increasingly authoritarian politics and ethical absolutism of the Papacy. These were centuries in which religious history, as opposed to ecclesiastical history, recorded great struggles of personal conscience in adapting to the new challenges of the Renaissance throughout Europe, finally culminating in Martin Luther's 95 THESES of 1517. Among history's choice ironies is that one of the richest historical periods of personal belief and struggle coincided with a Papacy dominated by Italian princes intent on collecting the very art and manuscripts which were raising serious questions among the educated laity, particularly those of the German towns. Hus was an early reformer, but the questions raised by his movement led to his burning at the stake ordered by the Council of Constance in 1415 - the same council which finally ended the scandal of the Great Schism (1378-1417) with its contest between Avignon and Rome as the papal seat and sadly amusing election of a third pope at the Council of Pisa in 1409 when reconciliation between the other two claimants proved impossible. But with the papal question solved, the teachings of Hus were back on center stage and Prague herself now lay open to charges of heresy and thus became the object of five Papal Crusades. Other events, more serious than Papal Crusades, however, emerged to alter the Central European legacy irrevocably.

With the capture of Constantinople by the Turks in 1453, profound cultural and political changes took place, though even this event did not intimidate Pope

Paul II from proclaiming yet another Crusade against the Bohemians in 1466. Of far greater significance, the Hapsburg-Turkish division of Europe began to emerge. To its credit in the midst of internal and external late fifteenth century turmoil, the city was able to solve its own problem of reconciliation between nobility and townspeople without setting off a war. Interestingly, the nobility retained the privilege of brewing beer while the town gained a greater measure of political autonomy - a balancing act not attained by the German states during the Reformation of the succeeding century which witnessed the clumsy solution of the Peace of Augsburg in 1555 allowing each ruler to dictate the religion of his people. The nobility-town agreement in Prague survived even the overlay of religion and politics of the Thirty Years War (1618-1648)[5] and the failure of the Hapsburg rulers to make either an absolute monarchy or a Catholic

[5] *Although the causes of the war were deep and complex, the precipitating event was the Defenestration of Prague when the Bohemians insulted envoys of the Holy Roman Empire by throwing them out a palace window. Fortunately, the envoys landed on a pile of dung which saved their lives if not their dignity.*

kingdom of the German states, principalities and cities. Four centuries later, the assassination of the heir to the throne of Austria-Hungary would lead to the Great War (1914-1918) of the twentieth century which finally ended the centuries-old Hapsburg drive for hegemony. With the capitulation of World War I, the last Hapsburg solution embodied in the 1867 founding of Austria-Hungary was exposed for what it was - a state not only an anachronism but a virtually incomprehensible historical relic from its inception. It could solve neither the problems of its own sizable minority populations nor play a consistent role on the international scene.

In these earlier centuries, however, the problem of hegemony seemed simpler, though hegemonic aims are never simple. A Succession Treaty in 1471 integrated the currently ruling House of Jagelonský in Hungary both with the Bohemian crown and with the House of Hapsburg, this time establishing a dynasty which became the basis for Hapsburg rule in Central Europe in one form or another until the 1914 assassination, which left only pretenders to a non-existent throne. Apparently also concluded with World War I was the six-century division of Eastern Europe between the Hapsburg and the Turkish (later Ottoman) Empires. In this case, appearance disguised reality. Now as the twentieth century approaches its end, the Eastern European division between relatively prosperous states and the lagging economies of others again mirrors the Hapsburg - Turkish division.

That division was unknown in its complexity as Prague, a dowager empress with many centuries behind her, now with the Czech-Hapsburg unity enjoyed her second Golden Age under Rudolph II (1576-1611), King of Bohemia and Hungary and Emperor of Rome. But hegemony, other than cultural, was never a long-term possibility for a small state in the center of Europe bounded by giants. That is a common opinion in the Czech Republic of today,[6] caught between Germany and Russia, in an area which has once again in the late twentieth century become a power vacuum. In the late sixteenth century, however, Rudolph II in choosing Prague as his residence made his court a brilliant center

[6] *Conversations with Dr. Marcel Preisler, August and September 1996.*

for the arts and sciences. Tycho Brahe and Jan Kepler belong to this era.

But Prague's second Golden Age was short-lived. The city's historical context changed with the Thirty Years War and resubjugation with a new constitution enforcing Catholicism and restricting town rights under the Hapsburg rulers Ferdinand II (1620-1637) and Ferdinand III (1637-1657). While the Peace of Westphalia of 1648 ended the war, it also ended (seemingly definitively at the time) Hapsburg hopes to dominate Europe. Meanwhile, the population of both Bohemia and Moravia had slumped to between one quarter and one third of its prewar level. The Thirty Years War left in its wake 270 devastated castles, and over 100 towns and 1100 villages shared the same fate.[7]

Continued postwar Hapsburg efforts to dominate the small Czech realms, years of Turkish wars, peasant tumults and a final epidemic of plague in 1713 point up dramatically the difficulties of these centuries. Amazingly, these same years saw the beginnings of a road net-

[7] *Krejčíř and Soják, 59.*

work and an opera house in Bohemia. In 1786 Mozart's opera, "The Marriage of Figaro," had its first international performance in Prague. Perhaps even more amazingly, the city took its modern shape of the four Prague towns in 1784: Staré Město (the Old Town), Nové Město (the New Town), Malá Strana (the Lesser Town or Minor Side) and Hradčany (the Castle District) - all integrated into a common administrative system with common authority.

These late eighteenth-century years also saw the 150-year extinction of Poland as it was successively divided among Prussia, Russia and Austria. The European center was hardly stable, but for the moment the power vacuum appeared filled. When Bohemia itself as part of the Austrian Empire came in 1848 to be ruled by the last of the Austrian monarchs, Franz Joseph I, there was no hint that his reign would end in 1916 amid the horrors of World War I nor that the conflict would lead to the founding of a modern Czech state. For those who could mull history, however, it was evident in the nineteenth century that liberalism had been defeated by nationalism and that the future appeared uncertain indeed.

When the twentieth century experience finally comes to an end with a new millennium, the tiny Czech state, known for a brief period as Czechoslovakia, in one century will have endured both Nazi and Communist domination, abandonment by the West with the Munich Pact of 1938 and a less-than-warm reception from the West in its struggle to escape the Communist legacy. But it will also justifiably take pride in Charter 77 asserting the liberal rights of the larger European tradition and the beginnings of a new civil society as the Soviet Union imploded. The enduring Czech legacy of the last two centuries will belong to the musicians Antonín Dvořák and Leoš Janáček, to the statesmen Thomas and Jan Masaryk and Václav Havel whose music and diplomacy healed what they could and held out hope when the city's people could only submit.

Not only did Prague's stones record all this history of the dowager empress city, but the stones also shared in the unique historical problem of periodization and many stones remain in their own periods today just as they were laid. Confronting periodization exposes the heart of history as interpretive. Issues of meaning and hierarchy illuminate the dialogic space between events and the human mind in which "history" happens. Turning now to view Prague from this aspect of periodization, we see that her beginnings hold the usual mix in cities' origins of legend and reality. According to one legend, a princess-diviner in the year 723 proclaimed "a vast city" on the banks of the Vltava River where only vast forest then stood. Twentieth-century archeological excavation places the construction of Prague Castle a century later in the second half of the ninth century, with the High Castle on the opposite side of the river dating roughly to the same period. Together these castles both protected and centered the new city on the Vltava.[8]

Hopelessly mixing history and legend is the story of "Good King Wenceslas" (Václav in the Czech language) whose famous square became in later centuries the site of numerous civic demonstrations. But when the historian examines carefully the early chronology of the Prague kings, even if Attila the Hun (434-453) is included, it is difficult to pinpoint who precisely was the king

[8] *Mráz, 16*

of legend. A Václav (Wenceslas), Knight of Bohemia, is described as ruling between 924 and 935, the assassination victim of his brother Boleslav I (935-972). Apparently the king of legend was this Knight of Bohemia. Thus legend enters history with the slaying of Wenceslas, later considered a martyr-saint but mentioned in Czech chronology only as the Knight of Bohemia who ruled between 924 and 935.[9]

The saintly king of legend, sanctified in the future, may have achieved this status merely by being assassinated. Nowhere does history seem to record the legend of the saintly king. But legends are real if not true, and the immense square in the center of modern Prague with its impressive equestrian statue of Wenceslas attests to the legend's continued viability. Interestingly, a work published during the Communist era places the murder and sanctification of "Good King Wenceslas" in 935: "As a Christian martyr he became the dauntless patron saint of the nation and the symbol of the state of Bohemia. Before long he began to appear on the rulers

[9] *Krejčíř and Soják, 11.*

(sic) seals and on Bohemian coins. The first Bohemian chorale was dedicated to St. Wenceslas: the crown of Bohemia was consecrated to him ..." [10]

The first Czech King, as opposed to a Knight of Bohemia, was Boleslav the Valiant (1003-1004), Knight of Poland, who captured and blinded the ruling Bohemian knight. Yet history also records that the first Czech sovereign, Vratislav II, was crowned in 1085 by grace of the German Emperor Henry IV (1056-1106) who, in the true fashion of Realpolitik, bestowed the Czech crown upon Vratislav for himself alone, not for the founding of a dynasty. In combination with the establishment of the Diocese of Prague in 973, this later crowning gave the city its recognition as a royal center.

There seems no way of reconciling the historical record as currently presented with Václav, son of Vratislav, reigning between 924 and 935 followed immediately by the reign of his brother Boleslav I (935-972), with

[10] *Mráz, 19. The first edition of this work was published in 1986, late in the Communist era (how late was obviously unknown at the time) with the first English translation appearing in 1988.*

the Boleslav of 1003 and the Vratislav placed on the throne by Henry IV in 1085 as the first Czech king. Standard Western histories of Europe usually omit the intricacies of Bohemian chronology, highlighting merely the Treaty of Verdun in 843 which divided the Carolingian Empire and the reign of Alfred the Great as King of Wessex beginning in 871. In the centuries under question here, Bohemia itself is simply considered as being reduced to a state of dependence by the German ruler Otto the Great (936-973). Subsequent comments on Bohemian history are subsumed under the expansion of the German realms checked in the fourteenth century as both Poland and Bohemia occupied their briefly significant moment in the wider history of Europe. This was for Bohemia, after all, the century of Charles IV.

Whatever we can or cannot make of these contradictions, legends remain real. When we encounter the customary periodization of Romanesque through Modern, we learn that the first historical records date from the tenth century,[11] confirming the archeological

[11] *Mráz, 18.*

evidence previously noted and also confirming historical reality by asserting that Boleslav I "who assassinated his brother Wenceslas" [12] was visited by a Jewish merchant, Ibrahim ibn Ya'cub, in 965 en route to the court of the Germanic Emperor Otto I. While this event fits our earlier chronology, there is nowhere any mention of Wenceslas as "good King Wenceslas." Nor does being Knight of Bohemia constitute holding the crown of Bohemia and Moravia, the ancient Czech lands.

When we examine the Romanesque city, however, we seem to be more firmly rooted in the less slippery ground of history. Viewed from the aspect of periodization, by the twelfth century Prague's culture was based on the Latin West, making the Bohemian realms part of the vague yet once again real "Christendom." Likewise by the end of this century, Prague had begun to assume at least part of its modern shape completed, as we have seen, in the eighteenth century. But the districts we know today as the Old Town and the Castle District had clearly emerged as early as the twelfth century. The ancient

[12] *Mráz, 19.*

stones began to form an extensive settlement on the banks of the Vltava. Central to Romanesque Prague was the Old Town Square, holding then the historical treasures still in existence including the Týn House for foreign merchants and to the north a considerable Jewish settlement which eventually became part of the city in its own right. Perhaps fittingly, because historical periodizations emerge only slowly, Mráz summarizes the period under consideration in words which the dowager empress city might find a bit deprecating if not downright offensive: "To say that Romanesque Prague was truly a city is to exaggerate slightly. It must be realized that Prague was at the time not a town in the medieval sense of the word, for it possessed no town charter, no administration of its own nor any walls. There was no continuous built-up area, (sic) it only provided the framework and focal points of the subsequent Gothic town." [13]

As we enter the Gothic period, we find another Wenceslas I, the son of Přemysl Otakar I, ruling between

[13] *Mráz, 30.*

1230 and 1253.[14] What seems more significant, however, than efforts to separate the inseparable history and legend is to focus on the vast social and economic changes which permeated this period of feudalism in its full development. In the Gothic period, we find that the Convent of St. Agnes was the first Gothic building erected in Bohemia, a full century later than the origins of the Gothic style in France. What is known today as the Lesser Town arose and the son of Wenceslas I, Přemysl Otakar II, became the first Bohemian King to win the crown of the Holy Roman Empire in the face of Hapsburg, Hungarian and Papal opposition. Town walls were built after 1231 and fortified, but today only the Powder Tower remains of the Old Town fortifications. As for the New Town, which held the main stretch of walls, thirteen towers and gateways testify both to the vulnerability of the city and to its thirteenth century importance. Because the Gothic walls followed the terrain of the city, they enclosed the old Romanesque

[14] *Mráz 28, 30. The historical answer probably lies in the fact that the saintly Wenceslas of legend was the Knight of Bohemia mentioned earlier, not King of the Czech lands.*

town unevenly. A characteristic that Prague did not share with other Gothic towns was its dual nature: the Lesser Town and the Old Town which enjoyed far more prestige and claimed the Charles Bridge, the Lesser Town banks and the foot of the Petřín Hill. Little remains today of the Gothic Lesser Town.

Little remains likewise of efforts to make Prague the center of a vast Central European empire - a project which geography alone easily prevents.[15] Under the last[16] of the Přemyslid dynasty which had ruled Prague for four centuries, Wenceslas II (1278-1305) consolidated Bohemia, married the daughter of the Polish king, thus gaining the crown of Poland, and won the Hungarian crown when that ruling dynasty died out. Such plans for greatness were foiled almost immediately, however, when Pope Boniface VIII (1294-1303) placed a member of the French House of Anjou on the throne of Hungary. Boniface was the last of the Roman Pontiffs to try to

[15] *Conversations with Dr. Marcel Preisler, August and September 1996.*

[16] *Condensations based on Mráz, 30-45.*

exert direct Church authority over secular rulers. The French government demanded his trial before a general council of the Church after his infamous bull, "Unam Sanctam" (1302) concluded: "We therefore say, declare and affirm that submission on the part of every man to the bishop of Rome is altogether necessary for salvation." [17]

Meanwhile, more pressing concerns occupied the rulers in Prague. To protect the city from the ever-present danger of flood, the actual ground level was raised an average of three or four feet. Gothic Prague was thus built literally over Romanesque Prague. Other defining features of Gothic Prague include economic prosperity, expansion of trade, growth of monasteries, establishment of at least twenty churches and finally around 1287 a unified town administration.[18] Prague's citizens contin-

[17] *McNeill, 334. Boniface was arrested in 1303 by an official of the French government in collaboration with the Pope's Italian enemies and died soon after that event, a broken man, his papal exertions in ruins and the loss of Church power evident for all to see.*

[18] *Krejčíř and Soják establish a much later date of 1784, 69.*

ued to push for political autonomy over the next three centuries. This was not to come, in spite of (or perhaps because of) increasing cultural links with Western Europe. The Hapsburg - Turkish divide of the future was clearly evident by the fifteenth century.

Prague's greatest period of a Golden Age, however, did not occur under the Hapsburgs. With Charles IV, as we have seen previously, the building of the Charles Bridge, the beginning of St. Vitus Cathedral and the privileged place reserved among the electors of the Empire for the King of Bohemia were all achieved.[19] Unfortunately, Charles' son Wenceslas IV (1378-1419), only eighteen years old at the time of his accession, managed to anger Church authorities and generally led a reign described as weak, marked by conflicts with the higher nobility and his eventual dethroning in 1400 by the Rhine Electors, further testimony to the dominance of the German states throughout this period.

The periodization of Czech history also allows us to see as a period in itself the inability of the Roman

[19] *Mráz, 76. cf. Krejčíř and Soják, 37 and McNeill, 335ff.*

Catholic Church to meet the spiritual needs of its people in the face of continuing authoritarianism exercised by the Roman Pontiff. These issues were larger than Bohemia, even though the Hussite Revolution cannot be underestimated in its pivotal importance among the first anti-feudal and significantly anti-authoritarian movements in Europe.[20] In religious history, the period of Hussite Prague was a direct antecedent to the Protestant Reformation almost exactly one hundred years in the future when educated German laypeople resisted the efforts of the Roman Catholic Church in the indulgence controversy and Martin Luther's own spiritual questioning led to the 95 THESES of 1517. Looking back from this perspective of the next century, it is evident that Hus also sought more satisfying spiritual help in confronting the new questions of individual judgment, Scripture vs. tradition, and changing views of justification. Hus first gained popular support through the

[20] *The connections between Renaisssance and Reformation implied throughout our considerations here were originally raised by Professor Emeritus William J. Bouwsma of the University of California at Berkeley.*

sermons he preached in the vernacular in Prague's Bethlehem Chapel founded by two Czech citizens precisely for this purpose. But use of the vernacular was still suspect at the time, whether for religious or secular purposes. As the Hussite movement grew, Hus established a center in Tábor in midsouthern Bohemia which quickly became perceived as a possible if not actual center of opposition to both church and state. As long as Hus retained the support of the Czech King, he was safe from ecclesiastical punishment. But when Hus broke with the King over the selling of indulgences, the same issue which horrified Luther one hundred years later, he and his movement were open to Church sanction. An era of Hussite Wars and Papal Crusades against the Czechs between 1419 and 1434 followed Hus' burning at the stake on 6 July 1415. In 1915 a magnificent Art Nouveau monument was erected in the Old Town Square to honor Hus on the 500th anniversary of his martyrdom. Whether we can consider Wenceslas a martyr at the hands of his brother is debatable. The martyrdom of Hus is not, a point finally conceded by the Roman Catholic Church at the Second Vatican Council 550 years later when the verdict against Hus was overturned. Of martyrdom and sanctity, there evidently was no mention by the Council. But when Soviet tanks moved into Prague in 1968 to end the Prague Spring experiment in liberal Communism, the monument to Hus was draped in the black of mourning.[21]

Although the people of Prague always remained divided in their opinions of Hus, Prague itself became the leader in 1421 of a core of royal towns opposing the Papal Crusades.[22] Eventually Prague gained from the Hussite Revolution. Permanent title was given by Emperor Sigismund (who also became King of Bohemia) to lands confiscated from the Church and only Czechs and Utraquists could hold offices.[23] On the other hand,

[21] *Tim Porter, PRAGUE: ART AND HISTORY (Prague, 1995), 30.*

[22] *Mráz, 82ff.*

[23] *Mráz, 83. Utraquists were members of the Roman Catholic Church who believed that both the wine and the bread should be consumed by the people, not merely by the priest, at what was known then and for centuries as the Holy Sacrifice of the Mass.*

art suffered during the wars, as it always does. St. Vitus Cathedral, while not destroyed, remained unfinished until the nineteenth century. By the Late Gothic period, however, both building and art work in Prague had resumed.

In the following fairly defined historical period, that of the Renaissance, we find that the medieval character of the town remained unchanged, although the Late Renaissance of the sixteenth century did witness the construction of streets, entire squares, castles, houses of the nobility and the intricate beauty of sgrafitto art. Mráz's opinion summarizes well the medieval character of the town, still visible in many parts of Prague today: "At core Prague remained a Gothic city below the Renaissance facade; it continued to live in gothically conceived buildings until the Baroque period." [24] Thus it is hardly surprising to see the Renaissance period in Prague considered an intermezzo. In light of the reign of Rudolph II (1566-1611), however, this is perhaps too harsh a judgment. Under Rudolph the city enjoyed its

[24] *Mráz, 99.*

second Golden Age, as we have seen: "It was no mere chance that at the Rudolphinian time the epithet 'Golden Prague' was used for the first time, as it reflected the glitter and magnificence of the Imperial Court in Prague and its magnificent art collections." [25] Mráz concludes broadly:

> The situation in Rudolph's Prague at the turn of the 16th to the 17th century was complicated; great contradictions maintained tension in the basically medieval town, drunk with the luxury of the Imperial Court, and imbued with German Lutheranism and the Spanish spirit of the Jesuits; it was a town in which various European languages were spoken. ... (with) the arrival of a new style (the Baroque) ... Prague experienced years of its most profound moral decline and highest artistic achievement.[26]

[25] *Mráz, 118.*

[26] *Mráz, 132.*

Foundation of Greater Moravian Empire

reign of Mojmír 1st (830 - 846)

His successor, Rostislav, invited the Byzantine missionaries - Constantine and Method in Moravia to help spread Christianity.

Assassination of Duke Václav

in 935 by the command of Boleslav, his brother

In his time, Václav was a well educated ruler. He implemented a number of changes in the sphere of foreign policy. He was later declared a saint and the patron of the Czech lands.

Foundation of Bishopric in Prague

in 973

The first monastery was founded by Mlada - the sister of the Czech duke Boleslav II. well before 970. In 1344, the Prague Bisphoric was granted the title of Archbisphoric.

Přemysl Otakar II

1253 - 1278, the King of Bohemia,
owing to his wealth and the strenght of his army;
he was awarded the title of "iron and gold" king

During his reign, he conquered the Austrian lands.
He was killed during the Battle at Moravian Field,
against the Roman king Rudolf of Hapsburg.

Assassination of Václav III

in 1306; (1305 - 1306) the King of Bohemia and Hungary

He was assassinated in Olomouc during his campaign for Poland. The purpose of the campaign was to preserve the Polish Crown. Thus, in 1306, the House of Premyslids, which was under the Czech throne for more than 400 years, crumbled.

Charles IV

1346 - 1378, King of Bohemia, Emperor of Rome, the period of his reign is referred to as "the golden age of art"

He became the most significant European ruler in his time. To his credit, the Czech State witnessed unprecedented development, and hence consolidated itself as a country independent of the German Empire. He is primarily known for his support for art, architecture, literature and the Church (the foundation of a university in Prague, construction of castles, cathedrals, etc.).

Master Jan Hus

Catholic preacher of the commons

He preached the reformation of the Christendom, and since his views and the ideas of the Catholic Church differed considerably, he was burned to death at the stake as a heretic on July 6th, 1415.

Jan Žižka of Trocnov

follower of the teaching of Jan Hus, from 1419 till his death in 1424 was the commander during the Hussite wars against the Catholic nobility

Rudolph II

1576 - 1611, King of Bohemia and Hungary, Emperor of Rome, his reign is reffered to as "the golden age" of Czech literature

Prague became a center for European science and art.

IOHAN-AMOS COMENIVS, MORAVVS. A° ÆTAT

Jan Amos Comenius

1592 - 1670;

also called "the Preceptor of the Nations"

As a result of the recatholisation, he emigrated from the Czech lands. He was the originator of modern pedagogy. He tried to implement more amusing methods of teaching at schools as well as other reforms pertaining to schools.

Thirty Years' War

1618 - 1648, a long conflict between the Czech non-Catholic nobility and the Hapsburgs, which soon escalated into an all-European clash

After the defeat of the Czech noble army in the Battle of the White Mountain, the Czech lands witnessed a process of re-catholisation. The war ended after a Westphalian Treaty was signed, which disabled the Hapsburgs from winning control over Europe.

Maria Theresa

1740 - 1780, Queen of Bohemia and Hungary, Empress of Rome

Through a system of reforms she strove to place the Hapsburg state among the developed European Great Powers. She introduced compulsory school attendance and paid attention to the development of both agriculture and industry. By these liberal changes she contributed to the latter abolishment of servitude in the Czech lands.

1918

Foundation of independent Czechoslovakia

28th October 1918

This achievement was preceded by the Pittsburgh Treaty, which approved the integration of the Czechs and Slovaks into an independent country. T. G. Masaryk was elected President of the republic (1918 - 1935).

Occupation of Czechoslovakia by the German forces

15th March 1939

Protectorate Bohemia and Moravia was established. Slovakia under the influence of Germany proclaimed independence as a republic. Most of Czechoslovakia was freed in May 1945 by the Soviet Army, the remaining parts by the American troops.

DUBČEK + HAVEL

"Velvet Revolution"

November 1989

Long - lasting internal political tension culminated into mighty protests led by students heralded also by other citizens against the Communist regime. The leadership of the Communist Party was abolished and Václav Havel was elected President of the republic.

Meanwhile, with the dying out of yet another Czech line, the Jagellons, Hapsburg power now embraced much of Europe. In 1527 Ferdinand I (1526-1564) was elected King of Bohemia.[27] Hapsburg power continued to dominate Europe even with the eventual division of the vast realms between Austrian and Spanish dominions when Charles V (1519-1556) of Spain abdicated in 1556, leaving his kingdom to his son Philip II of Spain (1556-1598) and his brother Ferdinand. With Rudolph II's (1576-1611) gaining of the Hungarian crown and the cession to him by his brother of the Austrian Lands, the great empire on the Danube which had been only a dream for early Czech rulers now became a reality for the Hapsburgs. As for Bohemia, we have seen that the Hapsburgs were to rule it and much of Central Europe until the Great War of 1914-1918.

In the sixteenth century, it is readily comprehensible why the Bohemians gave their support to the Hapsburg ruler Ferdinand. Because Ferdinand was a Catholic, the automatic assumption appears to have been

[27] *Krejčíř and Soják, 49.*

that he would reach an accommodation with the Church in Rome. Likewise, Ferdinand seemed to offer a buffer against Turkish incursions. Dreams of any accommodation with Rome were unfulfilled as the Council of Trent (1545-1563) erected a figurative doctrinal and disciplinary prison for the Church which alienated European intellectuals, if not entire populaces, for at least the following two centuries, indeed until the present. Wars of religion in France and the seeming impossibility of separating politics from religion finally led to the Thirty Years War (1618-1648) of the following century, as we have seen in our brief survey of highlights of Czech history. It may be worth remembering also at this point that the precipitating event of that war was the Defenestration of Prague, certainly a unique way of disposing of enemies or unwanted persons. There have been three defenestrations in Czech history: in the Hussite wars, at the beginning of the Thirty Years War, and with the advent of a Communist regime in the twentieth century. The third was undoubtedly the most traumatic for the state. Jan Masaryk, son of the founder of twentieth century Czechoslovakia, held out for democracy against

Communist pressure for as long as he could. When he "fell" from a window, the democratic problem he posed for the Communists was ended but their explanation of suicide was never accepted.

For the Prague of an earlier age, the Baroque period began with the victory of the Hapsburgs discussed above and with the Counter-Reformation, as well. In the following century, the overlay of political and religious issues literally engulfing Europe dragged the Czech realms into the Thirty Years War, as we have seen. Ironically, we can see from this vantage point how one event can interact with the historical issue of periodization to define an entire era. For the Czech realms, one battle of the Thirty Years War at Bílá Hora (White Mountain) outside Prague in 1620 decided the succeeding 300 years of history - a remarkable example of periodization forced by events. Prague and most of the Czech cities surrendered to the Catholic forces without fighting and the Catholic victory was celebrated as a "miracle." Now the remaining "heretics" were forced to accept Roman Catholicism and the Jesuits established the Clementinum from the original monastery church of St. Clement to lead the expansion of the Counter-Reformation eastward. The Hapsburg emperor determined to curb both the power of the Bohemian towns and the political freedom of the nobility. As witness to this assertion of Hapsburg dominance, twenty-seven leaders of the anti-Hapsburg Defenestration and uprising which had started the Thirty Years War were executed in the Old Town Square in 1621.[28] Their twenty-seven white cobblestone crosses on black backgrounds laid into the pavement of the Old Town Square remain today one of the most moving sights the city offers. By the end of the Thirty Years War, Prague had lost two thirds of her population and stood half deserted with thousands of looted homes. Ironically again, these very conditions aided the rise of Baroque art, leading into another distinct period in the history of the dowager empress city.

Noble palaces graced the rebuilt parts of the city. Largely through the efforts of a Burgundian painter, Jean Baptiste Mathey, the city's architecture began to acquire a precision and harmony of proportions in vivid contrast

[28] *Krejčíř and Soják, 55f.; Mráz, 137f.; Hill, 124f.*

to the extravagance of Early Baroque architecture.[29] In viewing Prague today, there are few structures more magnificent than the High Baroque Church of St. Nicholas in the Lesser Town Square. The visitor's entire being seems pulled upward as in a Gothic cathedral, a far more difficult feat with the tendency toward grandness and exaggerated decoration typical of the Baroque style. Building activity in Prague intensfied in the eighteenth century in the period of High Baroque, including the first placing of statues on the Charles Bridge. The changing face of the city was now more profoundly evident than anything the Renaissance had accomplished. Architects adapted churches, monasteries, palaces and town houses in the rounded style of the Baroque and Prague literally became a Baroque city.

A consideration of Prague as a Baroque city also highlights the "playing with" dates characteristic of the Late Baroque period, and this explication in itself opens another door to the consciousness with which Prague viewed its own past. As the Gothic period succeeded

[29] *Porter, 58ff; Mráz, 154ff.*

the Romanesque, Gothic dates were still expressed in Roman numerals. It was considered virtually a blasphemy to "play with" lettering. For example, the Powder Tower (Late Gothic) used the rigid form of the lettering as an uninterrupted ornament. The same caveat regarding lettering applied to the Early Renaissance period. Early Baroque also respected the basic forms of Roman lettering, exemplified in the sign over the entrance to the City Hall, "Prague, the Head of the Kingdom." By the Late Baroque period, however, (c. 1700-1800) every architectural form was used to "play with" and leave the message of the exact date in an attention-getting way. For example, a Baroque lettering cryptogram appears on the statue of St. Augustine on the Charles Bridge. The text DOCTORUM PRINCIPI was used to give the full message of the year, DoCtorVM prInCIpI, i.e., DCVMICII (500 + 100 + 5 + 1000 + 1 + 100 + 1 + 1), (MDCCVIII, 1708). Hence no further "date" of erection was needed. The Late Baroque "Black Death" column near St. Nicholas Church in the Lesser Town carries a similar cryptogram of the year.[30]

This same period viewed politically was the Age of Maria Theresa (1740-1780). Once again the peace of Europe was shattered at the beginning of her long reign in the disastrous war with Frederick II of Prussia who refused to honor the Pragmatic Sanction of 1740 and seized Silesia, thus triggering the War of the Austrian Succession. But the Theresan administrative reforms affected Prague in a far deeper way than the war. Maria Theresa established Provincial Deputations for Bohemia and Moravia with authorities in both areas introducing a new taxation system. A Supreme Judicial Court in Vienna was established, education advanced, and in 1750 a new unitary currency issued for all the Hapsburg lands. Towns were deprived of their ancient right of proclaiming capital sentences, a first census was taken and the Seven Years War sought to reacquire Silesia, a goal unattained within a war which encompassed most of Europe and the North American Colonies, as well, where it was known as the French and Indian War (1756-63).

[30] *I am much indebted to Jasan Burin, M.S., practicing architect and Visiting Associate Professor of Architecture at the University of South Carolina at Clemson, for these insights.*

By the death of Maria Theresa and the accession of her son Joseph II (1780-1790), Prague had become Germanized in significant ways. Whereas the town had retained its Bohemian character until the eighteenth century, now both nobles and burghers used German as their language. Only the rural people retained Czech, and when they moved into Prague, the city became divided along lines of language and nationality. But it is also worth remembering once again in the midst of these eighteenth century changes that Mozart found acknowledgement in Prague as nowhere else in Europe and that in the Prague of the Enlightenment, music held a dominant place.

When the French Revolution of 1789 engulfed all of Europe and the Napoleonic Era followed, the nineteenth century became one of Prague's most difficult eras. Population stagnated, the economy declined as an indirect effect of the Napoleonic wars and Bohemia continued to be part of the Austrian Empire. An odd pairing emerged for the city. On the one hand, after 1867 it became part of the Austro-Hungarian Empire, the anachronistic state mentioned earlier; on the other hand, the widespread nationalism of the period led to a Czech revival, just as it created national mythologies and folklore throughout many of the "subject nationalities" of Europe. By the middle of the nineteenth century, it was clear that nationalism had won out over liberalism (both born in their modern form during the French Revolution) and that the Europe of the future would be divided along national lines carrying ominous undertones of superiority and inferiority, and introducing yet another period into Czech history. The Czech Revival in this nationalistic century meant for the arts a time of particularly great fertility, "of joyful enthusiasm, stimulated by the rebirth of hopes" [31] ended all too soon with the occupation of Prague by the Prussians in 1866 as Bismarck pursued his plans for German unification through war.

In the last years of the nineteenth century and the beginning of the twentieth century, the faded dowager empress city became a large industrial center, though no equal to the German cities. Prague constructed new bridges to link the parts of the city divided by the Vltava,

[31] *Mráz, 209.*

and the Art Nouveau style showed one of its finest works in the Hus monument which we have already mentioned. Twentieth-century Prague became the city of Franz Kafka, who seemed to foresee not only Prague's future but that of Europe itself in his strange and disturbing works. At the same time, however, Czech townspeople continued to take a major role in pursuing liberal and democratic aims. This same combination of liberalism and democracy was to make the newly-created Czechoslovakia of the twentieth century the only Central European nation to preserve a democracy between the world wars. Then Czechoslovakia, deserted by its allies with the Munich Pact of 1938, came under Nazi domination; but even after World War II ended, it was the last of the Central and Eastern European nations to fall into Stalin's domain.

Unfortunate developments abound during the Communist rule of 1948-1989. Certainly the failure of the Prague Spring in 1968 must rank high on a list of national tragedies anywhere. From our vantage point at the end of the twentieth century, we can see that the reforms sought then under Alexander Dubček were strikingly similar to those which Mikhail Gorbachev later tried in the Soviet Union, only to preside over the death of the state he tried to reform. Not the least of the physical and psychological defacements of Prague and her people during the Communist era was the construction of towering apartment complexes around the rim of the ancient city, a construction prevented from even greater expansion and architectural damage only by lack of funds. The outskirts of Prague today bear a disconcerting similarity to the present-day outskirts of St. Petersburg and Moscow. What these latter two cities lack, however, is the unreconstructed combination of Romanesque, Gothic and Baroque styles in their magnificent setting on the Vltava River. Spared Nazi bombing in World War II, Prague today appears to a greater degree than many European cities much as it always has. Today the Czech Republic, separated from Slovakia since 1993, is among the most promising of the states in Central Europe and Prague herself a proud old empress.

But what purpose does this periodization and unavoidable revisiting of historical highlights serve? Certainly it situates Prague within the larger European scene, highlighting both differences and similarities of Czech culture over the centuries and the seemingly-endless Hapsburg struggle for domination. Periodization also situates Prague in a religious perspective which the focus on events cannot do of itself. Perhaps most significantly, periodization can lead us more clearly to patterns the historian can deduce from the history of the ancient and beautiful dowager empress city which a mere chronology of important events cannot do. Periodization is pattern-making of its very nature. Why refer to Prague as a dowager empress? What patterns of Czech history emerge and what do the stones of Prague tell us of symbolism and meaning? Questions of such a nature have no definitive answer, but we can learn much from closely examining both patterns and stones--two of the least likely pairings a historian might make.

A pattern which emerges virtually consistently over the centuries is embodied in underlying antagonisms within the society itself. Czech against German is only one of the more obvious of these antagonisms. In a Central Europe long dominated by Germanic kings, Bohemia remained a small state and a latecomer on the fringe of the Holy Roman Empire. Even then, it was drawn inexorably into the religious conflicts of the sixteenth and seventeenth centuries. In an atmosphere "saturated with religion,"[32] it is perhaps more surprising than not that the religious wars of these centuries failed to destroy the small Bohemian state. Destruction of a state is one thing, however, and subjugation another. The Czech state could not escape the Hapsburgs. Even with the final dissolution of the Holy Roman Empire after the ending of the Thirty Years War with the Peace of Westphalia in 1648 and the Hapsburg failure to reform the German states as Catholic, the dynasty endured. But as we have seen, the Hussite Revolution was central to demolishing the institution of "Christendom" if not of Hapsburg pretensions to rule a Catholic Europe.

As leaders of the first coherent and theologically based revolt against the Roman Catholic Church, the Czechs obviously benefitted from the spectacle the Church itself presented in the Great Schism, with the scandals of the Renaissance Papacy following closely

[32] *The phrase is William Bouwsma's.*

after. It is important to note at this point two additional patterns within this larger pattern of Czech vs. German and both against the Papacy: Czech opposition to authoritarianism of any kind and the struggle with the meaning of "church." The Hussite Revolution was grounded in opposition to the authoritarian theology of Augustine, thus melding well with political movements for more local autonomy. In each case, authoritarianism was the enemy, though Hus himself became both a symbol and a shield for reformers far more radical than he. In the following century, the Lutheran Reformation played an even more significant role in the proliferation of extremist religious groups from Anabaptists to millennarians. Although it is a misreading of history to assume that Church abuses caused the Protestant Reformation of the sixteenth century, certainly abuses played their part. In the case of Bohemia, the wealth of the clergy and nobility formed a stark contrast to the poverty of most Bohemians. The authoritarianism of the Roman Church was displayed prominently when Prague was placed under interdict and Hus excommunicated before his burning at the stake. Nor does Second Vatican Council recognition of error in the 1960s correct that error. Burning at the stake might be in itself considered a pattern of the period, carried out most viciously in the Spanish Inquisition.

Behind the issue of Church authoritarianism, however, was another pattern of greater significance which remains so to the present: how to define "church." An institutional definition is obvious, but this was not the question raised by either Hus or Luther, or by Hus' predecessor John Wyclif. The issue was salvation for the faithful in another life. It is not within the scope of this book to elucidate the doctrinal differences among Hus, Luther and Calvin nor the dynastic issue which brought the definitive break with Catholicism in the England of Henry VIII. It is, however, within our intellectual province to point out that Bohemia, however fringelike it was to the Holy Roman Empire, played a highly significant role in the beginnings of the religious reformations and redefinitions of "church" in the fifteenth, sixteenth and seventeenth centuries. In the case of Hus, religious sentiment blended with the honor of Bohemia.[33] With the death of Hus, Bohemian reformers became more militant, more Utraquist in their theology and ever more keenly aware of the spiritual bankruptcy of the Catholic Church in its Crusades against them. As might be expected, not all Bohemians supported the Utraquist theology, but a 1483 Utraquist uprising in Prague was instructive for the future when the Catholic nobility failed to support the king. Of all the reformist divisions, the Hussite followers at Tábor remained the most vital.[34]

Nevertheless, with the Turks invading Southern Europe, it was to everyone's advantage to reach a compromise, if not an agreement, on religious matters. What happened instead was a pattern of religious warfare, evident in the series of religious wars in France, culminating in the Massacre of St. Bartholomew's Day in 1572, finally settled (though only for a time) by the accession of Henri of Navarre as Henri IV in 1589. Religion permeated the Thirty Years War, as well, and Prague was referred to as the "Jewel of the Catholic Reformation"

[33] *Griffin, Prague lectures.*

[34] *Griffin, Prague lectures.*

after the Peace of Westphalia in 1648. Prague was a reluctant jewel. In Bohemia, only one-third of the population continued to embrace Catholicism and in Prague less than 5% adhered to the traditional faith.[35] With the Council of Trent and mobilization of the Jesuits to combat further anti-Papal movements, the era of religious wars both accelerated briefly then declined virtually everywhere by the end of the seventeenth century. The rise of major nation-states under strong, centralizing monarchies and the Scientific Revolution of the seventeenth century gave the final push to the secularization movement which had been the product of centuries. It is again worth noting that these centuries saw a pattern of complex interplay with the Thirty Years War, the Tridentine Reform, the Papal "shock troops" of the Jesuits, and the Hapsburg ascendancy. Thus it is important to recognize another pattern implicit in these events: the underlying Czech-German antagonism was linked to the political and religious struggles of the fifteenth and sixteenth centuries.

[35] *Griffin, Prague lectures.*

The issue of Utraquism, though long dead, brings up another pattern in Czech history. We have already noted the spiritual bankruptcy of the Roman Catholic Church during these centuries, but the Renaissance itself had led to another political-religious issue, heightened two centuries later with the Scientific Revolution. In using private judgment as a norm in religious matters, the question of an end-point arises. The issue evokes a Nietzschean world in which we can see where an all-embracing relativism could lead. Yet who is to fear the self-conquering Ubermensch of Nietzsche? On the contrary, he is to be admired. Or is it only his perversion in the Nazi racial doctrine of the Superman that we fear? The late twentieth century has not yet found an answer to the pattern of private judgment and total relativism, and under what conditions, if any, a state could survive such a chasm. The Postmodern landscape of dissolution and Deconstruction at least provides fertile ground to pose this question. And spiritual bankruptcy is hardly a new phenomenon in the recorded human experience known as history.

A political pattern likewise emerges from another confluence of religion and politics over these centuries. The Hapsburg territory may have been simply too large to govern effectively under the conditions of the time which lacked readily available communication links. On the other hand, reminiscent of Russian and Chinese peasants who go their way today as they have for centuries with central authorities far away in distance and thought, the Hapsburg emperors could not be everywhere in their realms when dissent linked itself to religious belief. A land too large to govern at all may be the ultimate political anachronism. It occupies so much geographical space and attention that there may be no room for the more complex phenomenon of political space in which identity establishes power, applicable to a Hapsburg emperor as much as to a Bohemian farmer.

Other related political patterns emerge from the Thirty Years War. The Treaty of 1648 brought the collapse of the Holy Roman Empire and the final failure of the Hapsburgs to make a Germany either absolutist or Catholic. For the Bohemians, the intricate political interplay of Trent, the Jesuits and the Hapsburgs brought a temporary submersion, if not a total loss, of their identity. The small Czech state was simply too tiny to play a major role in the new era of the nation-state. Other and different patterns could undoubtedly be deduced from the history of Bohemia. But there are few cities in which the very stones of the streets speak its patterns. It is time to read the language of cobblestone.

The stones of Prague come in three sizes: large paving stones for vehicular street traffic; medium-size trident stones for horses not only in the entryway to the Great Hall of the palace where medieval jousts were held, but in obscure places within the city as in the present shortcut to the Metro stop of Anděl; and finally small paving stones used on sidewalks for people. Each tells its story, even in these brief identifications. All these stones have recorded the chronology and periodization we have seen as history. The stones' size and placement in castle, bridge, side street, shortcut give both meaning and perspective in ways the historian can read. One example among many is the Charles Bridge with its combination of "traffic" and "people" stones. The large paving stones, with their bridge of more recent statues, have been in place since the fourteenth century. Along both sides of the bridge, smaller stones offer a surrogate home to the artists, aspiring artists and con artists who have always competed in the ancient human game of the marketplace. In the romanticism of the Charles Bridge illuminated at night, both historian and casual bypasser can wonder at the poetry of love, meeting and parting, which the stones hold. Human feet have felt these stones for centuries and human hands have thrown them at political adversaries in times of anger and frustration. Whereas horse traffic throughout the city is now only for the tourist, centuries of horses and carriages have passed over this bridge now barred mercifully, and in full accord with the Czech sense of history, from automobile traffic.

Other bridges crossing the Vltava to link the two shores of the city have endured the abuse of blood and gunpowder, urine and gasoline, pollution and automobiles - the kitchen middens of civilization set in stone. And over all is the absent-yet-present figure of Charles IV, whose greatness needed but one word on his tomb: "Karel." When historians write of the importance of perspective, they usually refer to the ability to situate oneself and one's society in a present world of other societies and to see one's own past not as past but as constantly being relived within us. The Charles Bridge incorporates both dimensions, in its twelfth century tower preserved within the "new" fourteenth century structure and in the people who live in Prague and those who come simply to see the dowager empress city. A perspective is both a place of vision and a place of beginning.

Past met present most recently in 1989 in the relatively bloodless "Velvet Revolution" against Soviet rule, now seen as not so velvet with a law of "Lustrace"[36] to ferret out in virtually endless secret police files all who "cooperated" with the Communist regime. Such a law is so lacking in perspective as to be devoid of

[36] *Chad Bryant, book review of Tina Rosenberg's THE HAUNTED LAND: FACING EUROPE'S GHOSTS AFTER COMMUNISM, (New York, 1995). Book review in the NEWSLETTER OF THE CENTER FOR SLAVIC AND EAST EUROPEAN STUDIES (Berkeley, Fall 1996), 3-5. The NEW YORK TIMES consistently refers to the law of lustration.*

either vision or beginning in the single-minded quest for vengeance. Even President Havel has not been above suspicion.

Yet in the teeming and almost impenetrable by-ways of the Old Town, the stones continue to record history and the musical language of the people, aware of their musical heritage, but perhaps not so aware of how their language itself carries that heritage. We have spoken previously of the twenty-seven stone crosses laid into the pavement of the Old Town Square, placed near both the city offices and Prague's astronomical clock. While the stones commemorate the dead, the clock is a constant reminder of time, life and mortality. Beyond the Old Town Square is the Jewish Quarter, once a ghetto. The gravestones of the old Jewish cemetery tell their own story. Each person buried in the cemetery has an individual stone, with thousands of people buried in layers twelve feet deep. To touch this ground and to see these gravestones, with nests of smaller petition and remembrance stones placed there by visitors, is to touch the sacred. And perhaps only very aged persons and cities can be considered "sacred" in the late twentieth century-hence, at last, the meaning of Prague as a dowager empress whose ongoing reign depends only upon her somehow sacred presence.

Silently speaking their truth, the stones carry deep meaning for present residents of Prague[37] who can narrate a lifetime spanning both Nazi and Communist regimes. One Czech citizen spoke eloquently of his preference for birth either in the seventeenth or in the twenty-second century. Fearing the lack of a similar sense of history among the youth of the society, he knows what all historians know: that a majority of any people can at any time be mobilized by another Hitler to vote for a latter-day Third Reich. So the city's stones become haunted too by the Sudetenland Germans and the Munich Agreement which is still referred to by many in Prague as "the peace treaty we had with Hitler." Thus was Prague spared.

Through the centuries of spiritual and political struggles which, hopefully, we have made live again in

[37] *Dr. Marcel Preisler, Jaroslava Preislerová, Carla Montie, Karen Bauer and their circles of friends.*

these pages, the stones' story remains--highlighting, periodizing and patterning an ancient history. Bohemia likewise remains, peripheral still to world conflicts in the last years of the twentieth century. What can never be peripheral is Prague, the dowager empress of culture and wisdom. By enduring and witnessing over many centuries, "always here and always now," Prague continually recalls for us a sense of history and a mortality somehow sacred. Anything in any society can be a carrier of meaning. I walked very slowly up the hill at this parting.

BIBLIOGRAPHY

PRIMARY SOURCES

Extensive personal visits to Prague in the summers of 1995 and 1996.

Participation in Denmark's International Faculty Development Seminar in 1995, with a request to chair a section on "National Sovereignty, Human Rights, and the Minority Issue: The View from Central Europe," in the Prague sections of the Seminar.

Participation in Oxford's University Vacations Programme. London, 1996. Seminar 700: "Prague: The Jewel of Bohemia."

Oral history interviews and conversations with Dr. Marcel Preisler, Jaroslava Preislerová, Laurence Oppenheim, Jasan Burin, M.S., Carla Montie, Karen Bauer and their circles of friends.

Special thanks to Jim Conlon, Director of the Sophia Center at Holy Names College, Oakland, for information on Juliana of Norwich and to William J. Bouwsma, Professor Emeritus at the University of California at Berkeley, scholar and friend.

I am much indebted to Jasan Burin, M.S., practicing architect and Visiting Associate Professor of Architecture at the University of South Carolina at Clemson, for his insights.

SECONDARY SOURCES

Bílková, Hana. A PHOTOGRAPHIC GUIDE TO PRAGUE. Prague: Artfoto Publishers, 1995.

Bryant, Chad. Book Review. (Rosenberg, Tina. THE HAUNTED LAND: FACING EUROPE'S GHOSTS AFTER COMMUNISM. New York: Random House, 1995). Berkeley: NEWSLETTER OF THE CENTER FOR SLAVIC AND EAST EUROPEAN STUDIES, Fall 1996.

Griffin, Peter. Oxford University. Seminar lectures for Oxford University Programme 700. Prague: The Jewel of Bohemia, Charles University, 1-7 September 1996. London: University Vacations, 1996.

Krejčíř, Jaroslav and Stanislav Soják.
CZECH HISTORY. Prague: INFOA, 1995.

Mráz, Bohumír. PRAGUE: THE HEART OF EUROPE. Prague: Adventinum, 1992.

Porter, Tim. PRAGUE: ART AND HISTORY. Prague: Flow East, 1995.

The Stones of Prague
History, Pattern and Memory

AUTHOR: Mary R. Anderson

ILLUSTRATOR: Zdeněk Netopil

PUBLISHED BY: © INFOA
Address:
INFOA, Nová 141
789 72 Dubicko, Czech Republic
internet: www.infoa.cz
e-mail: infoa@ova.pvtnet.cz

Typeset in INFOA
Printed in the Czech Republic by
Moravské tiskárny a.s.,
Tiskárna Olomouc
Studentská 5, 771 64 Olomouc

ISBN: 80-7240-032-0